Stay Sweet.

ISBN: 9781792840487

SUPER SWEET
COLORING BOOK

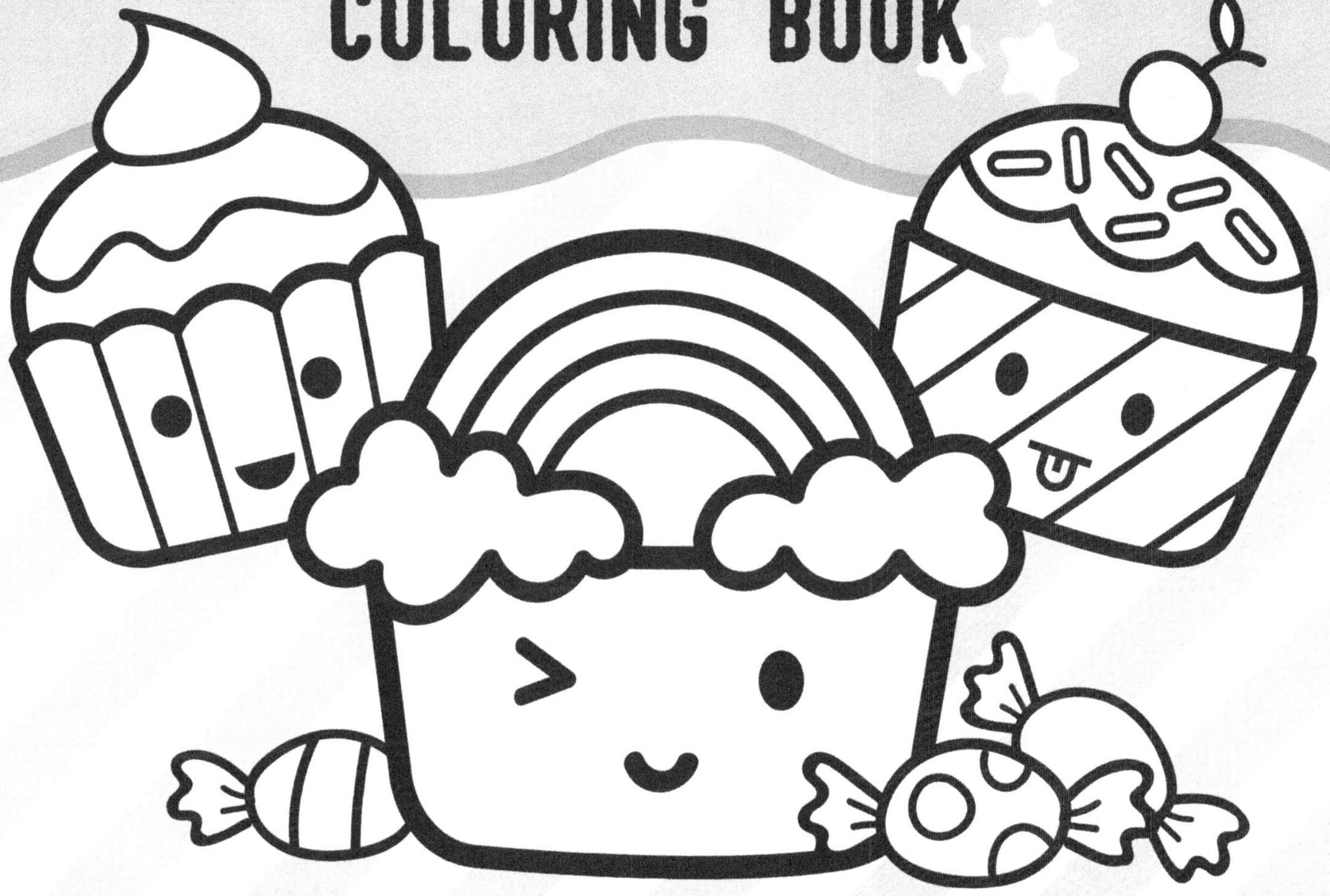

A COLORING IS RAD PRODUCTION

YUMMY.

U R RAD
LUV YA!
HUGS
COOL
LUV BUG

Sweetness
IS MY
Weakness.

U R
RAD
HUGS
COOL
LUV
BUG
FOR
YOU
U R
RAD
LUV
BUG
LUV
YA!

Be Cool.

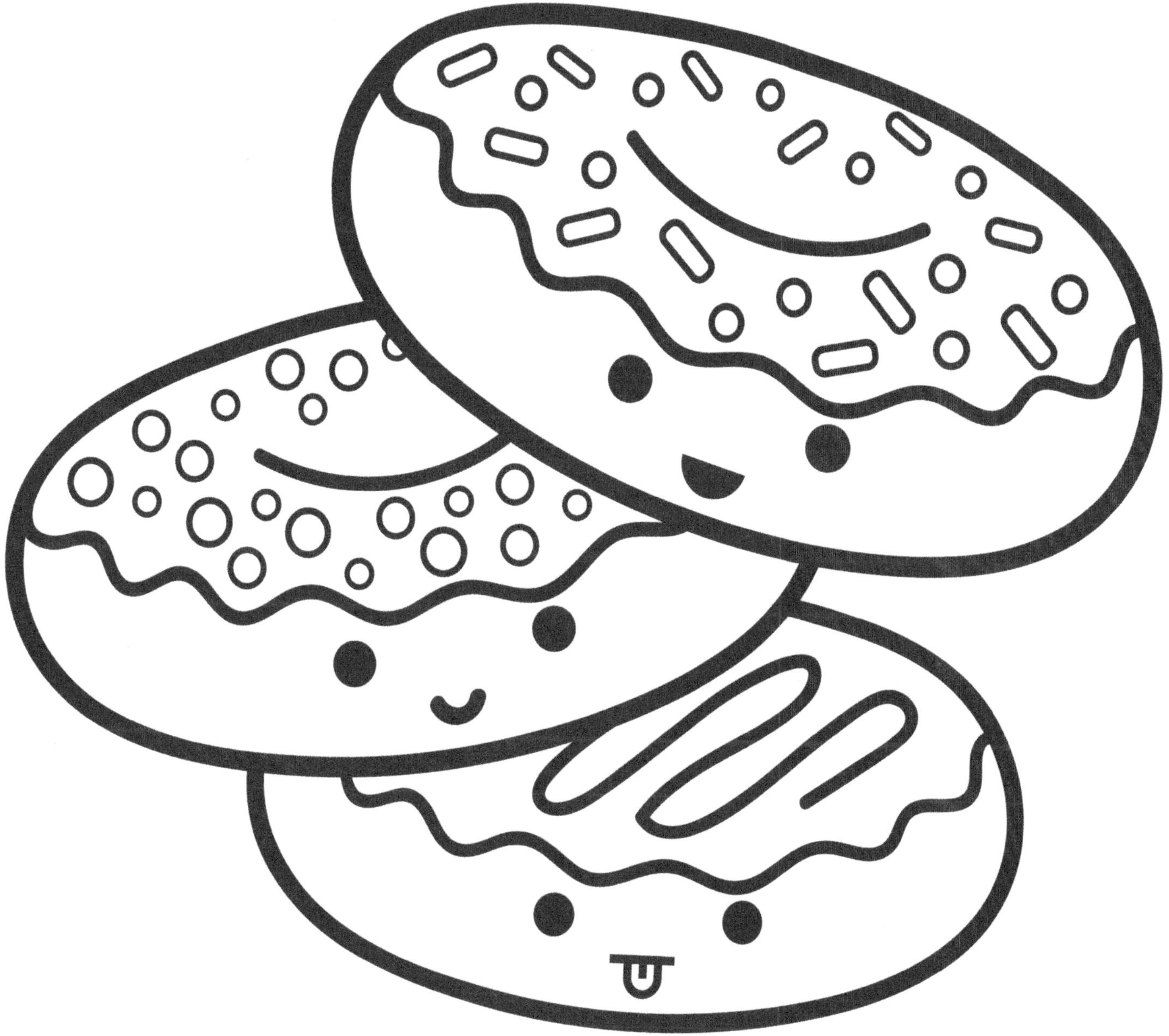

Sweet
Dreams.

Made in the USA
Monee, IL
09 December 2024

73088595R00031